T0258428

GADZOOKS!

Extraterrestrial Guide to Love, Wisdom and Happiness

Z-MAN

New Atlantean Press
Santa Fe, New Mexico

Gad·zooks (gad zo͞oks′, -zo͝oks′)
interjection
⟦< *God's hooks*, nails of the Cross⟧
Exclamation used to express surprise
or as a mild oath
[archaic or humorous]

Topics

GADZOOKS!
Extraterrestrial Guide to Love, Wisdom and Happiness

by Z-MAN

Cover Illustration: Mary Ann Salomone
Text Illustrations: Damiana Sage Miller

Publisher's Cataloging-in-Publication
Miller, Neil Z.
    Gadzooks! : extraterrestrial guide to love, wisdom and happiness / Z-man. -- 1st ed.
    p. cm.
    ISBN 1-881217-21-3
    LCCN 2001-087035

    1. Human-alien encounters--Poetry. 2. Unidentified flying objects--Poetry. 3. Spirituality--Poetry. I. Title.

PS3563.I41918G33 2001   811'.54
                QBI01-700178

Printed in the United States of America

Published by:
New Atlantean Press
PO Box 9638
Santa Fe, NM 87504

TABLE

Introduction

Hello,

I am Z-MAN—Mr. Z to some of you, a mystery to others. Actually, I am not all that mysterious. For example, I live with my wife and two children in a pleasant home located in northern New Mexico. Other members of our family include Walter, our hyperactive dog, Magic and Mini-Magic, our audacious cats, and Pepper our bunny.

I mention this because many people will want to know something about me and how I came to write this book. It all began during a beautiful autumn day in October. I was going about my daily business when several lines of strange and amazing poetry suddenly filled my mind. At first I was astonished because I did not comprehend this unusual experience. Where were the poems coming from?

The first poem that I received was a private communication informing me that whole generations of children are being raised without moral and spiritual guidelines. Benevolent extraterrestrials—the true authors of this poetry—wished to provide direction, and were offering me an opportunity to participate. I was free to accept or reject their offer.

I prayed to God for guidance and concluded that despite some unanswered questions, the poems are beneficial. The lyrics contain nuggets of wisdom that transcend cultural and religious barriers. Therefore, I am delighted to share them with you. I hope you enjoy the pictures as well; my daughter is the illustrator.

—Z-MAN

All Aboard

Gadzooks! I think I lost a screw.
I hear things in my head.
Now I'm sure there is a crew
Of E.T.s there instead.

They say I am their cosmic host,
Their earthly scribe as well,
And that it's time to make the most
Of what they have to tell:

Hello, dear friends, we're "out-a-sight"
And come from far away.
As messengers of God's great light
We have a lot to say.

He asked us to elucidate
The nature of your being
By having us illuminate
The strange things we keep seeing.

We observe you make the claim
"I want to change my ways."
But then you stay the very same
For days and days and days.

You may smoke or drink or curse,
Perhaps you laugh at friends.
Then you say, "It could be worse."
Of course, this all depends.

From our view up on our ships
The Earth appears in trouble.
Everyone must come to grips
And change things on the double.

Share your love with everyone,
For this you may not hoard.
Now buckle up, get set for fun.
We welcome all aboard!

Creatures Large and Small

Animals of the planet Earth
Are friends of ours, indeed.
They possess tremendous worth
Beyond all human need.

Some can read your every thought,
And know what's on your mind.
A few may even think you ought
To try and be more kind.

They respect you in good measure,
You are loved and feared.
And though they are a living treasure
Some have disappeared.

A few are savvy and may seek
To trick you with their skills.
Even those that are quite meek
Evoke their share of thrills.

Remember, though, that every creature
Upon the land and sea,
Is a very special teacher
With a similar plea:

"We can live among each other,
Adapting as we go.
The Earth is our blessed mother,
She loves her children so.

"Please treat us with your full respect,
Be thoughtful, kind, and fair.
And if you can, please help protect
The forests, streams, and air.

"Our planet is a special place,
With room enough for all—
Members of the human race
And creatures large and small."

Birthdays

A Cheerful Cluck

Neil's mama said she laid an egg
And he was incubated.
Of course she liked to pull his leg
And said he was related

To a chicken on the range—
His nose was like a beak.
She claimed he was a bit too strange
And that he should not speak

About the way he entered life;
It was a family strain
And caused a lot of inner strife
To raise a young bird-brain.

Later, when Neil flew the coop
And grew into a man,
His wife was privy to the scoop
And gathered his whole clan.

She questioned them about the day
They claim that he was hatched.
They didn't have a lot to say,
And no one's story matched.

Now his family says they checked
And think his wife is sick.
They also say he is henpecked
But was the cutest chick.

So on his birthday every year
They sing his favorite song:
"Happy Bird-Day" brings a tear
That lasts the whole day long.

You, too, have a sacred date
Decreed by more than luck.
So be sure to celebrate
With a cheerful cluck.

*Your body
is a work of art.*

Bodies

A Well-Maintained Physique

Your body is a vessel pure,
It's yours and yours alone.
You live within and must endure
Each cut and broken bone.

But did you know that every ache
And scratch upon your skin
Reveals the choices that you make
From somewhere deep within?

Your body is a traveling van,
A way to move about.
Of course, there is a lifelong ban
On getting in and out.

Except at night when you're asleep,
You sometimes park the car
And travel in your astral jeep
To a distant star.

Your body is a work of art;
A movie, show, and play.
Only *you* create your part,
So what will you display?

Your body is all this and more,
An organ of the earth,
Six billion that you can't ignore;
Each one has innate worth.

So when you meet some "body" new,
Reflect on what you learned:
Every "body" must be true
To what its soul has yearned.

And everyone, you must agree
Likes to be unique.
And, of course, we like to see
A well-maintained physique!

Living Hell

"I'm the one who saw it first!"
"You're a lying dog."
"I'm convinced that you're the worst."
"You live in a fog."

Quarrels cause a lot of pain—
A sign of disrespect.
There is little one can gain
By "proving" who's correct.

Treat your partner like a chum,
A pal who's really nice.
Most disputes are truly dumb,
So heed my cool advice:

Freeze your speech before you say,
"You are a heartless witch!"
Warm up to a better way—
Pretend you have an itch.

Scratch away each frosty thought.
Shake off your anger, too.
Then remember what you sought
To say to you-know-who.

It wasn't meant to hurt or sting.
How did your thoughts explode?
Can you now bring everything
Into a calmer mode?

Yes, your needs should be expressed;
They clarify your growth.
No one's thoughts should be repressed
So take this sacred oath:

When I'm inflamed, I will recite
"I promise not to yell."
Then a spark will not ignite
Into a living hell.

I Love You—Yes, I Do

When children wail, "I want that thing!
I want that thing right now."
Parents often fail to bring
Perspective to the "how."

How to say, "No, no, my dear,
It's not a proper toy,"
Even though it's very clear
It's sought by every boy.

How to say "I think that maybe
We ought to talk some more.
You are my favorite beanie baby,
Not found in any store."

How to say "I love you lots.
Let's take a walk today.
You and I can count the dots
All along the way."

Children need a parent who
Is more than just a bank.
They need a person just like you—
A grown-up they can thank:

"Thank you for the time we spend
Sitting by the creek.
I love it when we play pretend
And games like hide-and-seek.

"Thank you for the love you give
Each and every day.
It makes my life a joy to live;
I'll now grow up okay.

"For when you guide me firm and strong
With hugs and kisses too,
I swear I will not turn out wrong.
I love you—yes, I do!"

DISAVOW A LIFE OF
ROMAN TERROR.

Control

Roman Terror

Gladiators who fought in Rome
To prove their virile might
Were also just as fierce at home
Where they ruled with cruel delight.

"Obey me!" was a common theme—
A threat that harm was near.
Even mates with self-esteem
Paid homage to their fear.

Frightened wives would try to ease
The strain of raging moods.
Often they would try to please
Their men with special foods.

He enjoyed a hearty meal,
She his scarce affection.
This was their unspoken deal
Each day without objection.

Later, when the kingdom fell
And soldiers died in pain,
It ended the ungodly spell
Cast over the terrain.

At first, the women were confused
And didn't feel quite whole.
Remember, they had been abused
By men in full control.

Today, the patterns are the same
In homes where men are boss.
So, women, if your so-called flame
Assails you and is cross,

Find a way to leave him now
Or risk a long-lived error.
Take control and disavow
A life of Roman terror.

Journeys to Paradise

Sleepy Beatrice took a nap
And entered worlds unreal
Where she was caught within a trap
To be somebody's meal.

She cried aloud for all to hear:
"Please send a helping hand!"
Bea was shaking in great fear
And did not understand

Why she was now in a tree
Talking to a bird
Until her new friend said to Bea,
"Dreams are not absurd.

"They reveal so many things
About your state of mind.
Now, hop upon my outstretched wings
If you would be so kind.

"I want to take you far away
To a land of make-believe
Where everyone is hard at play
And gets what they conceive.

"If you are scared in the waking stage
Your dreams may trap you down.
And if you have a lot of rage
You may be kicked from town.

"But if you're happy as a lark
Like me, your winged soul
Your dreams will match your inner spark,
Lighting up your evening stroll.

"So remember me before you doze
Hold on to my advice:
Create your dreams to presuppose
Journeys to paradise."

Evolution

For Goodness' Sake

Long ago, before the Earth
Was formed into a rock,
God decreed "I shall give birth
To a cosmic clock.

"It shall last one billion years
Including day and night."
And as the twilight ever nears
It's time to set things right

About the fish, the bird, the ape
The human and beyond;
There is life in every shape
That came from Darwin's pond.

All emerged from a single cell
One species to a form.
Evolution works so well,
But Creation is the norm.

Bodies are the aftermath
Of natural law and order.
They follow a selective path,
And provide a constant border.

But life would be a crying shame
If souls could not fend death;
The reason your eternal flame
Was born from His One Breath.

Parallel paths of form and essence,
Science and belief.
These are your evolving lessons
Much to His relief.

Since bulk and core were made by God
His image is at stake
So try to be a pleasant clod—
Grow up, for goodness' sake!

Fairy Dust

Santa is a jolly man
And quite a chimney sweep.
Tooth Fairy has a dental plan
That pays while you're asleep.

Easter Bunny paints an egg
For every girl and boy
While hungry folks who have to beg
Are told to end their ploy.

The substance of what you believe
Is clad in mass denial
Designed to alter and deceive
Your plain and natural style.

Some beliefs are wholly true,
Derived from clear perception,
While others have a colored hue
That leads to self-deception.

How, then, can you learn to form
Perceptions that are real,
When fabrication is the norm
And bias has appeal?

Begin with children in your care,
Devoid of all pretense.
They will believe the lies you share
At everyone's expense.

Such false beliefs can hinder growth
And veil the greater truth.
So make a pledge, a simple oath,
Be honest with your youth.

Although all children are divine,
They need adults to trust.
Of course, some make-believe is fine
So spread the fairy dust.

*Greatness comes
from deep within.*

Majesty

Royal Heir

Midas had a golden touch
King Lear was quite insane
The Queen of Hearts demanded much
The Pharaoh was too vain.

Cinderella had a prince
Snow White had one, too.
There hasn't been another since
With quite the charm to woo.

True royalty does not exist
Within a family name.
Majesty, we must insist,
Has naught to do with fame.

Dignity and inner grace
Are virtues of the mind—
Qualities the human race
Is searching hard to find.

A palace seems the place to look
To make a man a king,
Or within a fairy book
Where dreams cause hearts to sing.

But greatness comes from deep within
Grandeur is yours to show
In spite of your unseemly kin
And who else you may know.

Therefore, stand tall and shout aloud,
"I Am Nobility!"
And you will rise above the crowd
For everyone to see.

Support your claim with noble deeds
And you are almost there,
A member of exalted breeds—
A real-life royal heir.

Good
is all
around.

Perspectives

Good with Grit

Awkward Annie banged her knee;
The pain was awfully bad.
It was a small emergency
Yet somehow she was glad.

She knew it could have been much worse,
A broken leg or two.
Then she'd need a full-time nurse
To see her whole day through.

So instead of crying out
At her poor run of luck,
She kissed her knee and raced about
To show her gutsy pluck.

The lesson that she learned from this
Is one she's cherished since:
It's true that from a simple kiss
Some frogs become a prince.

Another time Ann had a fight
With her dearest friend
Who claimed Ann failed to see the light
And that this was the end.

Ann ached because her heart was broke,
At times she'd even weep,
Until she had a brilliant stroke
Of insight fathoms deep.

She saw that bad was good inside,
That good was all around
And that her friend could be her guide,
Their break-up wisdom found.

Ann was happy with their bond
And wiser from their split—
The reason she will now respond
That bad is good with grit.

Discover your
life theme.

Prayer

God's Scheme

Suzy Goodheart prays each day
And goes to church as well.
She reads the Bible like a play
For God is really swell.

"Sometimes," she says, "God heeds my plea;
Sometimes He does not hear.
God is such a mystery;
Perhaps I was not clear.

"So I pray with greater stress
Upon the things I need.
Yet, He rarely seems to bless
Or satisfy my greed."

Maybe God will not dispense
His goodwill on your lives
Until you start to make some sense
Regarding inner drives.

Then God will surely cheer you on
And root for you to win
Even when it seems He's gone—
The game plan sort of thin.

He is nearby with all His grace
Prepared to steal the show.
You merely have to set your pace
And paddle with the flow.

Prayer is not a magic trick
Despite what you may think,
Even though God heals the sick
And is your spiritual link.

You must seek to find your role,
Discover your life theme.
This should be your constant goal:
Pray to join God's scheme.

Profanities

Sugar and Fudge

Frankie Foul-Mouth took a hike;
The dang trail was not clear.
So he rode his freakin' bike
To see his gosh-darn dear.

He said to her, "I have to say,
My mouth is full of spit."
She said to him, "That's quite okay,
It's usually full of...wit."

He laughed and laughed at her fine joke
Until he thought it through:
"I can make a jackass choke
With just a word or two."

Then he asked, "What's in a name,
A sound, a tone, or pitch?
My girlfriend is a pleasant dame
Except when she's a...witch.

"Excuse me, please, I can be crude;
My tongue is in the gutter.
And even though I'm one cool dude
I shouldn't have to utter

"Dirty slang to let you know
How pissed I seem to be.
Oh my gosh, there I go—
So many swears in me!

"Now I pledge to make a change
And speak with due respect.
My girlfriend finds it awfully strange
But loves my dialect."

Society is better chaste
Without a vulgar smudge.
So sweeten up your current taste
With lots of "sugar" and "fudge."

Let fair play
be your guide.

Responsibility

Payback Is So Sweet

When you make a big mistake
And want to keep your pride
Do the right thing, for God's sake:
Let fair play be your guide.

You may want to hide your face
And wallow in your shame,
But that would be a worse disgrace
Than taking the full blame.

Perhaps you broke what someone built,
Or smashed into a car.
Now you must admit your guilt
To avoid a karmic scar.

For when you lie about your role
In causing a misdeed,
You fall into a self-made hole—
Your honor starts to bleed.

If the blood is not contained
By mending all your cuts,
A loss of heart is preordained
Until you have the guts

To say, "I was the one at fault
And want to make amends.
That is the way that I was taught;
It helps me to stay friends

With everyone whose path I cross."
This can't be overstated:
*An obligation's not a loss
When dishonor is abated.*

So climb out of the hole you dug,
Stand up on your two feet.
I have a new cliché to plug:
"Payback is so sweet."

Smart-Ass

"Your mama's papa wears a wig,"
Mocked Bart, the carping cad.
"And your sister is a pig,
Who looks just like your dad.

"Our neighbor is a nutcase,
You tripped, so take a bow.
That purebred is a mutt-face.
The milkman lost his cow."

Egad! Bart has a piercing tongue;
It's sharp, as you can see.
Be careful that you don't get stung
By how he likes to "bee."

Some wisecracks may seem funny
When they betray a truth.
But like a nose that's runny
Should be wiped from the uncouth.

For when you speak of others
With mean, derisive quips,
You criticize your brothers
With venom from your lips.

No one should be harried,
And no one should be teased.
The burden that is carried
Is one that must be eased.

For the weight of scornful talk
Is on the taunting fool,
And your friends will take a walk
When they see that you're uncool.

With your countless wisecrack jeers,
And a temper that is crass,
You'll become among your peers
A genuine smart-ass.

You are the master
of your life.

Self-Esteem

Glowing Star

"Please sign my card in pen and ink,"
Cooed Lisa "Fan-of-Gold."
"Sign it now before I think
About your public mold.

"You stand for things I don't respect
And are a bad role model.
I know I really should reject
Some stars I choose to coddle.

"Instead, I wish to shout aloud,
'I met the well-known snob!'
You know, I'm not a bit too proud
To say, 'Be still, heartthrob.'"

Lisa has low self-esteem,
Her values are astray.
Actors are not who they seem
But bound by who they play.

So when you watch your next big show
Remember what you've seen.
A film star's autograph, you know
Is on the larger screen.

And when you next request a pen
To sign upon a line,
Remember what we taught you when
Your life was seeming fine.

You are the master of your life,
You are a model man.
You are the very finest wife,
You are your greatest fan.

Be the best that you can be;
Be pleased with who you are.
Express your full identity:
You are a glowing star!

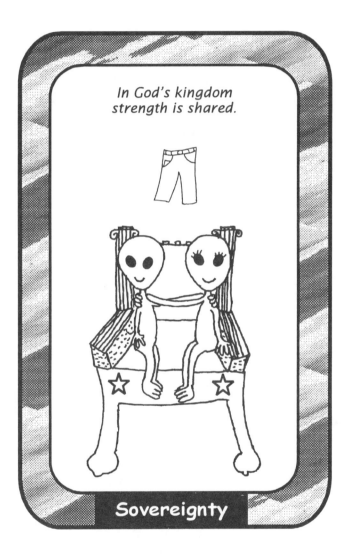

In God's kingdom strength is shared.

Sovereignty

Chief Pretense

Jack told his wife, "I wear the pants!
Within our family tree."
She said, "Please stop your silly rants
And maybe I'll agree."

"Thank you, dear. I won't be cross;
You are so very sweet.
Of course, I still must be the boss;
I'll try to be discreet."

She stared with wide-eyed mock chagrin
At Jack's attempt to flatter.
Then she said, "I'll let you win
On things that do not matter."

Very smart, this wife of Jack's;
She loses when she must.
It seemed as though *she* wore the slacks;
His game plan was a bust.

"Honey pie, I think you know
How much this means to me.
I beg of you, please try to show
Your deference to my plea."

"Oh, king of kings," she then declared,
"You are my leading man.
But in God's kingdom strength is shared;
It is His royal plan.

"So if you'll treat me like a queen
Upon a golden throne
A pair of pants won't come between
Two sweethearts home alone."

Because she was Jack's lovely bride
And made a lot of sense,
He dropped his trousers by his side
To end his chief pretense.

Children need a mom and dad who are not children too.

Teenage Pregnancy

Baby Whore

Marriage is a sacred vow
Reserved for mates in love
And couples who are learning how
To align with those above.

The goal is to achieve a bond
That grows in strength each year,
A love that ventures far beyond
Desire, lust, and fear.

Raising kids without this pact
Between a girl and boy,
Will become a juggling act
That no one will enjoy.

So be a happy clown instead—
Bring joy to the "unbearable."
You have a lot of love to spread,
The truth is not so terrible.

Children need a mom and dad
Who are not children too.
We know you will be awfully sad,
So adopt a larger view.

Later, when you're old and wise
And look back on your choice,
You probably will roll your eyes
And say in a clear voice:

"I'm glad I waited to raise kids
Until I was mature.
My boyfriend and I had big ids
But now I know for sure

"That marriage is a stepping stone
To family life and more,
And I would rather live alone
Than be a baby whore."

E.T.'s Farewell

LOVE, STRENGTH & LIBERTY

*Please move
beyond the past.*

Civilization

Another Time

It's time for us to say good-bye;
E.T.s must now go home.
But first we want to tell you why
There was a Fall of Rome.

A rich and mighty nation-state
Lost sight of God's decree
To go forth and emulate
Love, strength, and liberty.

Instead, the people took these gifts
And flipped them inside out.
Their love turned into sordid rifts
And strength became a rout.

But freedom took the greatest hit
And chaos followed suit
When everyone avowed that it
Must be absolute.

New laws were made to safeguard power
While civil claims were stalled.
This was not your finest hour;
The whole world was appalled.

This nation-state was now too sick
To stop its own decline.
But we declare that if you're quick
You still have time to shine.

Though cycles come and can repeat
And "Rome" has been recast,
We offer you a worthy feat:
To move beyond the past.

So practice what we preach in poem;
There's reason to our rhyme.
And though E.T.s must now go home,
We'll come another time.

Share your love
with everyone.

Family Photo

UFOs
(Uncommon Final Observations)

Introduction:
★ The author believes that benevolent extra-terrestrials wish to communicate with humanity.
★ Everyone needs to be more loving so that positive transformations can occur.
★ These poems provide a lyrical blueprint for achieving virtuous self-expression.

Animals:
★ Animals possess inherent worth and should be treated with respect.

Birthdays:
★ Birthdays are meant to be festive occasions.
★ Birthdays are sacred events; your existence is significant.
★ "Cheerful cluck" has two meanings.

Bodies:
★ The body is a vessel that each person occupies—an instrument for moving about on the Earth.
★ The body and its occupant are bound as a single unit. However, during sleep the occupant can leave its body to explore other realms.

★ Every "body," including its physical structure, ailments, cuts and broken bones, is a combination and reflection of the owner's desires—an outer portrayal of inner dynamics.

★ Everyone likes to be distinctive and uses their body for creative self-expression.

★ Everyone likes to look at an attractive body.

Conflict:

★ Arguments cause pain. They result from a lack of respect.

Conscious Parenting:

★ Conscious parenting requires your love of and dedication to the process of child-rearing.

Control:

★ Women must take control of their own lives and end any relationship where the man is domineering and oppressive.

★ Men who see some aspect of the "gladiator" in themselves must gain control over and refine their own aggressive tendencies.

Dreams:

★ There is a synergistic relationship between your waking life and dreams.

★ Dreams reflect inner desires and other aspects of your present state of mind; dream images (like the bird) represent facets of your own nature.

Evolution:
★ Theories of Evolution and Creation both have merit; they coexist without contradiction.
★ Human existence consists of a body and a soul. The body is subject to physical law; the soul is an extension of God.
★ Bodies, and the souls that inhabit them, follow parallel but distinct paths of development.
★ "Evolution" has two meanings: 1) the gradual development and enhancement of organic structures through natural law, culminating in more refined bodies, and 2) spiritual growth—becoming a "better" or more virtuous person.
★ Since you were made in the image of God, conduct yourself in a manner befitting of a supreme being.
★ "Clod" has two meanings.

False Beliefs:
★ Some of your beliefs are not true; they are cloaked in group denial—lies that society believes—contributing to your own fallacies.
★ "Bias has appeal" refers to your unconscious personal reasons for maintaining false beliefs.

★ Truth exists beyond all personal and collective lies; clarity is attainable.

★ Honesty and fantasy both have merit; each can be expressed in a healthy manner.

Majesty:

★ Dignity and inner grace are virtuous traits that you or anyone else can cultivate.

★ Your attitude and deeds determine your majesty.

Perspectives:

★ You always have options regarding how to perceive challenging events.

★ There's merit in maintaining a positive attitude; "dire" situations contain hidden benefits.

Prayer:

★ Seeking to have personal desires satisfied is an incorrect and selfish use of prayer.

★ God supports your efforts when you are clear about your larger and more meaningful goals. (God helps those who help themselves.)

Profanities:

★ Cursing is disrespectful.

★ A wholesome society is better than a vulgar one.

★ "Sugar" and "fudge" are substitutes for curses.

Responsibility:

★ Be fair and honest in all of your dealings.

★ Take responsibility for your actions.

★ Obligations are spiritual opportunities.

Sarcasm:

★ Wisecracks are not funny.

★ You are accountable for your actions; they help define who you are choosing to become.

Self-Esteem:

★ "Public mold" has two meanings.

★ Some of the people that you revere may be undeserving of your admiration.

★ Idol worship mistakes the insignificant for true merit and is a symptom of low self-esteem.

★ Movies represent each actor's signature upon society. Celebrated performers have the potential to influence large numbers of people. As such, their civic responsibilities are immense. They need to be thoughtful and discriminating about the roles they play and how they choose to present themselves to the public.

★ Let your signature be a reminder that you are an important person with significant contributions to make. Focus on your own special identity. Be the best that you can be; there is a "star" within.

Sovereignty:

★ Marriage is a union of equals; there are no "bosses" in healthy relationships.

★ Treat your partner like royalty.

Teenage Pregnancy:

★ Marriage is a sacred vow between two people dedicated to the love and responsibilities of the relationship.

★ Sexual intercourse is best regarded as a divine commitment.

★ Ideally, children would be raised by mature and stable adults.

★ *Bring joy to the "unbearable."* has two meanings: 1) Don't despair over an unplanned pregnancy; there is a happy solution, and 2) The solution is to allow your child to be adopted by loving adults who are "unable to bear" their own children.

Farewell:

★ Your current civilization has many similarities to early Rome during its moral and spiritual decline.

★ History often repeats itself but this does not have to occur.

★ You can learn from your past and rise above adverse environmental and cultural conditions to create a utopian-like society.

A New Itinerary

Benevolent extraterrestrials have more to share with you. Please visit *www.thinktwice.com/gadzooks.htm* to read their updated messages. Look for their "far-out" wit and wisdom in future versions of **Gadzooks!** as well. Here are some of their planned topics of discussion:

Adolescence
Art
Astrology &
 Divination
Bible
Birth
Communication
Compassion
Courtesy
Cycles
Crime
Death
Diamonds
Diet
Drugs
Earth
Emotions
Extra-
 Terrestrials
Family
Friendship &
 Loyalty

Gluttony
Grace
Handicaps
Health
Heaven & Hell
History
Honesty
Independence
Jesus
Karma &
 Reincarnation
Law & Social
 Agreements
Love
Marriage
Math
Meaning
Meditation
Parties
Plants
Privacy
Prophecy

Reality
Reason
Risk
Sadness & Grief
Satan
School &
 Education
Science
Security
Seniority
Sex
Sharing
Sin
Skills
Time
Vacations
Vanity
War
Waste
Wealth & Greed
Wonderment
Work

Purchasing Information

Additional copies of **GADZOOKS!** *Extraterrestrial Guide to Love, Wisdom, and Happiness* (ISBN: 1881217-21-3) may be obtained from New Atlantean Press. Call 505-983-1856. Or send $9.95 (in U.S. funds), plus $3.50 shipping, to:

New Atlantean Press
PO Box 9638
Santa Fe, NM 87504
505-983-1856

email: global@thinktwice.com

Bookstores and Retail Buyers: Order from Baker & Taylor, Ingram, New Leaf, or your favorite wholesaler. Contact Midpoint Trade Books or New Atlantean Press for more information.

Individuals and Non-Storefront Buyers: Take a 40% discount with the purchase of 5 or more copies (multiply the total cost x .60). **Shipping:** Please add 7% ($3.50 minimum) for shipping. Checks must be drawn on a U.S. bank. Larger discounts are available.

FREE CATALOG: New Atlantean Press offers nearly 200 publications on holistic health, diet, natural immunity, progressive parenting, vaccine alternatives, inspiration and spiritual growth. Send for a free 32-page catalog. Or visit our website at: www.thinktwice.com/books.htm